Black Rhymes With A Reason

Henry Earl Oaks

ISBN: 978-81-19654-11-6

First Edition: 2024
Rs. 200/-

Cyberwit.net
HIG 45 Kaushambi Kunj, Kalindipuram
Allahabad - 211011 (U.P.) India
http://www.cyberwit.net
Tel: +(91) 9415091004
E-mail: info@cyberwit.net

DEDICATED TO

Daddy and Madea
John and Rosie Lee Oaks,
Who Still Exist, Somewhere in Time.

Contents

Because I'm A Fearless One

Even as my body rest and sleep,
My mind continues to wonder and weep.

Tossing and turning preparing in aguish and hurt,
Unable to comprehend the necessity to treat a small one like dirt.

When the curtain call and there is no more applause,
Others will stand in the shadows for the cause.

As I'm lowered six feet down,
Not even wearing a Crown.

I may not have the woman or gold,
I may be lucky to have my soul.

Still, I'll Wonder will they be safe and protected?
From predators who themselves may have been neglected.

However, that's no excuse for them to inflict abuse on someone to small to fight back,
How would they feel if they were under attack?
By some much larger sadistic beings of creation,
Looking for someone much smaller and weaker to vent their frustrations.

Fearless One

No matter what the consequences or the stakes.
I'm unafraid to come forward or even pick up the gun,
Because you see, I'm a fearless one!

There's some things a man will crawl thru hell to avenge or prevent.
It'll even veer him off the road of his life's intent.

This hurt and desire is stronger than the love for a mate,
Distinguishable by love and hate.

Lord let me burn in exchange for their safety and happiness,
But let the perpetrators burn with me.
You know I'm not afraid and I won't run,
Because you made me a fearless one!

Hail Queen Nzinga

In ah southwestern afrikan region
Ah tall strong ebony queen lead ah legion.

1656 wuz da third decade
Dat she and her warriors battled da slave trade,

Wit much Portuguese blood staining da soil
This war would not allow her people to be dare spoil.

While many Afrikans sold dare people 4 european goods,
Queen Nzinga and her warriors, ambushed them from da woods.

Mutha Afrika 1st

Mutha Afrika is da cradle of civilization,
From her womb sprang every nation.

Egyptian hieroglyphics stolen by greeks,
Egyptian blood diluted by arab sheiks.

Hannibal's conquest of Rome,
The Moors making Spain their home.

It all started in ah east afrikan paradise,
It ended dare kause what happened wasn't nice.

During dare permanent honeymoon blist,
All my great great granddaddy wanted was ah kiss.

But Mutha Afrika offered him mo' of her womb,
To persuade him to play ah different tune.

Kause da little one told her dey'd be bigga dan big,
All they both had to do wuz taste da fig.

Granddaddy got kicked outta his crib.
I bet he wish he'd kept his rib.

But den where would I be?
Mutha Afrika sprang forth me.

Marooned

Dey wanted me ta work da sugah cane fields,
So I run away to da Cockpit Country,
Dey don't come in dare kause da Maroons kill em.

Dem be my brothas,
I join em and fight.

We fight da Spanish in da 1500's,
Den come da Brit's 4 some Jamaican rum.

My chillen fight em in da 1600's,
Den dey chillen fight em in da 1700's,
Til dey give up and we win da war.

Where Is The Lord

Where ya at Lord, Where ya at?
They knocked me out Lord, they knocked me out.

Woke up in chains Lord, I woke up in chains,
Where ya at Lord, Where ya at?

Brought me up for air Lord, They brought me up for air,
All I could is see water Lord, all I could see is water.

Where ya at Lord, Where ya at?
I see land now Lord, I see land,
Puttin' me to work Lord, they puttin' me to work.

Where ya Lord? Where ya at?
Half of us died Lord, half of us died,
Kept me alive Lord, ya kept me alive.

But, still I ask… Where ya at Lord, Where ya at?

I'm Still Here

I've been pierced wit nails and needles and felt no pain,
I walk on water every time it rain.

I came from above, but I'm not a fallen,
I was sent down here on ah righteous callin'.

Now I'm just ah runaway slave with gun in hand,
With my cross hairs aimed at who they call the man.

Honkered down deep in the trenches,
My aim is blocked by bucks and bed wenches.

They think I'm their enemy as well as his,
Yet, when he abuse them, they always forgive.

But I don't have to abuse them,
Just my being alive is what they despise.
Like him they hate me and seek my demise.

N River

I'm a river of beds, I'm a river of streams,
But when you mispronounce me you can hear my screams.

I'm the River Niger from the continent you see,
I'm not a nigger brother, No that's not me.

It happened during the middle passage when they took you away,
They got the wording wrong and decided to let it stay.

Now you use it more than they do.
Is that what you think of yourself, or do you think what they say is true?

God made me calm to flow into the Atlantic,
The way you talk about me you sound like you're frantic.

You think it's amusing, and you say it for fun,
If one of them said it you'd wanna pull out a gun.

Neither are you a Negro, 'cause you're not from Spain.
It's Spanish for black, but it's still not your name.

Angel With A Broken Wing

Earthly woman hear my plead,
Earthly woman supply my need.
I must fly again,
I must soar again,
It doesn't matter how,
It doesn't matter when.
I have to get back home.

No earthly being can physically
Fix whut happened to me,
Still an attempt to try
Would be so heavenly.

After descending thru a multitude,
of nebulas,
I landed among physicians to exit
A womb.
I wasn't ready yet, so I grew up
Much too soon.

Hands on help is labor in vain,
It's love that's needed to lighten
the strain.
It'll mend my wing and I can fly again,
It'll mend my wing and I can soar again.

I'm far from home,
That's heaven above.

If you drain my life,
It'll poison my soul.
Leaving us both
distance and cold.

The evil down here is poison
To me,
It breaks my feathers like
like branches on a tree.

I came here to save you,
Risking us both being enslaved
You in your mind, and me in
a cave.

Help me to fly away,
And I'll take you with me.
We can both fly and soar,
If that's your desire,
Or you can burn forever in an
everlasting fire.
And I'll go as I came, Alone.

To help me back there,
You must express some love.

I reach out to you for comfort and hope,
Does your hatred for me
Match your love for dope?

Dishonest Abe

Yeah, Abe gave the Emancipation Proclamation,
Only he gave it reluctantly with much hesitation.

With slave labor fueling the confederate war machine,
He was compelled to do the most logical thing.

Even though Abe feared loosing the border States,
He knew that soon gray coats could be at the gates.

Why the news of Ole' Abe being elected,
Had caused the south to feel neglected.

So, they all seceded immediately,
With only twenty-three small states,
Abe appealed to them repeatedly.

It seems it was just not to be,
And as for Abe, I question his honesty.

Abolition, Revolution

They portrayed him as ah madman,
In all actuality he was ah sadman.

Disappointed in his government flaw,
In it's 1850 Fugitive Slave Law.

Considering quakers and the like to be soft.
This abolitionist was pissed off.

Bleeding Kansas was just a starter,
Three years later,
After Harper's Ferry John Brown became a martyr.

Split Down The Middle

Half went with Malcolm and W.E.B.
Half went with Martin and Booker T.

Division and anger started a new war,
It was soon forgotten what we were fighting for.

Oh Yeah! Freedom, freedom to choose how to be free,
As soon as that's settled we'll try it and see.

But oh my God! When will that be?
Two halves make a whole only with unity.

Brought Here

Brought here by way of the Atlantic,
Captured by my own brothers.

They sold me to foreigners,
The way Joseph's brother did millenniums before.

Should I hate them for what they did?
Or bless them the way he did?

There was famine in the homeland,
So, he sent them grain.

There's famine in the motherland,
So, I send them donations.

Though I may be blessed as Joseph was,
Still man… I was brought here.

I Feel Da Pain

Monsoon seasons
Has it's reasons.

It's H20
makes rice paddies gro.

And afta da rain
I feel da pain.

Afta da rain
We do our thang.

But somebody cut
My straps,
And my chute collapse.

It's all over for me
'til I land in a tree,
And I feel da pain.

I try to get down and flee,
But Charlie's all around me.

They march me a mile

And sho me da blood
Of a child.

Now I'm back in da rear,
Safe in Saigon.
Don't have to worry 'bout
da Viet Cong.

I no longer in Da Nang,
Yet, I still feel da pain.

I'm back in da world, back
from afar.
Only to witness an even
Stupider war.

The blood of more babies done
By their drive-byes,
Da scream of the young mutha
as she cries.

Such punks have no remorse.
As a matta of their own re-
course.

Still, any coward that murders
ah
Child has to be insane.......
as for me...again I feel da
pain.,

They it blame on me,
I say I'm not like that u see.
'Cause I feel the pain.

They let me go be 4,
Wantin' 2 know.
Dis not yo war.
So, what u fightin' it 4?

One Big Family

Lot's of brothas and sistas in this Family.

Some of them dark,
some of them light and
some of them in between.

One parent dark,
one parent light,
Still, they love each other.

It's a big family,
Vanilla caramel, coco, mocha,
walnut and chocolate.

Still, they're all black and they're family.

Fake Gangsta

Cap turned back, pants hangin' down,
Listenin' 2 dat hardcore sound.

Wanna be ah gangsta wanna be tough,
Committin' fratricide jest ain't enough.

Gotta be intelligent, and git hi scores,
In order 2 run Wall Street and banks off shores.

So quit flippin' n trippin' kause u ain't bad,
Yo ignorance and buffoonery is real sad.

Any punk can murder ah baby in ah drive-by,
Real gangstas shoot it out wit da cops, and they don't git hi

Fake ass mafiosa wanna be's lack you always,
Tryin' 2 emulate that homosyphillis Capone.
Git off his nuts and kulture and learn about your own.

Rather than join revolutionaries you'd rather see da pigs arrest us,
Even though our ancestors are cryin' out from da grave 4 justice.

Their legacy 2 u wuz dat u be ah nationalist patriot,
Yet u mock their dream wit your buffoonery and self hatred.

You remind me of nothing but dah manure of a maggot,
You're a spineless, gutless, lowdown, lowlife faggot.

The reason u hate women so much is cause u wanna be one,
Dats just ah facade wit da beeper, da gear and da gun.

Put u in ah 6 by 9, wit a lifer built lack ah ape,
Wit out yo gang banging buddies u wouldn't bust ah grape.

I still luv and wouldn't hurt ya, 'cause we share da same blood,
Just remember I'm highly explosive and you're just ah dud.

Labor Machines

We were once slaughtered by da millions,
It's not over 'cause it was done by civilians.

They still on us like Desert Storm,
What's the difference between a white sheet and a blue uniform.

Fattin' them walls and pack them in,
Industrialized exploitation ain't no sin.

Prisons the new plantation, so they're filled to the brim,
Crack fertilized Street so they don't get slim.

Job's for mo' kluckas to do their thang,
Stool pigeon sambo's still know how to sang.

I Must

Deep down inside of me,
Looms the essence of my soul.

I strain to spring forth
The intestinal fortitude
That encourages me To prevail

No intoxication can take control
No wine nor her nakedness.

I must be mesmerized only
By my Creator and His perfect will for me.

As he spoke me into existence
So must I speak it,
Then shall it manifest.

Let Me Back In

Let me back in
Let me invade yo system again.

I come phrom all ova da world,
Some call me boy, some call me girl.

As ah boy I wuz cultivated in da golden triangle,
Shipped in body bagz of dead G.I.'s wuz an angle.

I hit inner city streetz and I hit 'em hard,
I spreaded 2 suburbia n rural trailer parkz.

As ah girl I'm harvested in da junglez of Bolivia n Peru,
Dictatorz use my proceedz 2 equip dare troopz thankz 2 u.

Snort me, smoke me, shoot me, I don't care,
Jest as long as u let me back in dare.

Don't throw me away, or toss me aside,
You're angry, I hurt u, but dat's jest ya pride.

Jest let me back in,
You're da one who got greedy and committed ah sin.

I promise it'll be good dis time around,
Even if u don't smile u sure won't frown.

If u turn ya back on me now, I'll have 2 be sold cheap,
And eventually be decommissioned 2 da dung heap.

So, I ask u again,
Please, let me back in.

Challengin' God

People in Amerikkka be challengin' God,
Flouting arrogance to break His hod.

Thinkin' dat only da devil has ah wrath,
But even he's gonna be part ah da bloodbath.

Worshippin' idols and monuments of stone,
Like dat big white phallus at da capital's home

It violated many slaves and planted its seed,
In da minds of both offsprings who pursue greed.

God will meet da challenge, and drop them in ah lake of flames,
When He open da books, He won't see their names

Get Off Our Streets

Most of us don't want you in the hood
So git off our streets you invading virus,
You powered peckerwood.

Who brought you here, da CIA, da mafia,
Central and South American cartels, or da
Real conspiracy all the above?

Look whut you've done to our babies born addicted to you,
We shoulda destroyed your root before you grew.

Ruined careers, shattered dreams, lost jobs, lost souls,
broken spirits and broken home.
We must teach the next generation to leave you alone.

Gives It Up

Give it up buttercup, give it up,
It's making you soft as tissue.

The people you love are gonna miss you.

Ain't none of that crap no good,
It's just bringing down the neighborhood.

Give it all up,
If ya gonna quit screwing wit coco leaves,
dump Mary Jane too,
'Cause none of those S.O.B.'s gonna help you.

So what if forty ounces are legal,
And they drink wine in the cathedral,
It's about you and your life,
'Cause when it comes to you, they won't think twice.

Give it up buttercup, give it up.

Sky Light

Sky light, sky light,
Watchin' da boyz in da hood tonight.

Circling da entire globe,
Like a giant eye and ear lobe.

Checkin' out what's going down,
From da east coast to da Puget Sound.

Sky light, sky light,
We know ya up dare ere' night.

Even in da daylight saving time,
You're listening in, when we drop a dime.

You're ah cluster of microwaves,
Snoopin' down on middle eastern caves.

Go ahead and wack dem Shieks,
They exploit us 'cause they think we're freaks.

Sky light, sky light,
Industradized contract site.

Why don't ya watch da cocaine trail?
Is it 'cause it's you you'll have ta nail?

Time Change

Nuerons taking control of tachyons,
Moving backwards and forwards through time and space.

Stopping to change my faith and that of the human race.

What an awesome responsibility that wouldn't even make me God,
I should give it to Him, and just stay in my pod.

Keep It Moving

Blood stained trails of alfa males,
Clearing a path for the aftermath.

Beta offspring refuse to follow,
Weakening the bloodline for all to consume.

Bowed heads refusing to raise
Bent backs breaking,
No eye to eye, no eye for an eye.

One hand pointing at the next generation
The other holding up his trousers.

It's Time We Both Quit

You think you're not sprung,
You think you can function without some.
Blowin cigarette smoke in my face 'cause you're hooked on nicotine.
Holding a mug to your own face 'cause you're hooked on caffeine.

So what if you dumped KoKo,
You're still messin' with Mary Jane,
They both alter the chemistry of your brain.
One is just as seductive as the other,
You show more love for them than you do your mother.

You have the nerve to scold me,
Drinking is something I picked up from my family tree.
You see it's in the blood and, I can't shake it.
But, I'm not going to be like you, and try to fake it.

I've been hustling just of long as you,
I's time we both realize the game is thru.
It's not worth all of the scraping and striving.
It's time we both got sober and quit jiving.

Where Can I Go?

Comprehending chemical escapism as a state of mind,
Remaining in the same time, distance and space I ask.
Where can I go?

Peering thru the strongest telescope I observe the back of my head.
A parallel and alternate universe offers only more of the same.
Again, I ask, where can I go?

Even yonder sea castles and pillars of sand can turn to salt and blow in the wind,
Yet my expiration is merely a transformation,
whose soul lives whether doomed of blessed.
So once more I cry out, where can I go?

No chemical can alter what really exists,
Nor, can it change beyond perception.
Even speeding beyond M.C. squared only puts me ahead of brings me back.
Time wasted changes nothing.
Now, I demand to know, where can I go?

Like a book of mirrors, it all becomes so clear,
With conception comes arrival.
I have arrived.

Shootin' Hoops

Flying high behind the rock,
Soaring thru the air with it cocked.

I'm slamming, slamming,
Yeah, Baby Slamming it.

In the playground after school,
Half court jumpers looking cool.

Swush baby swush,
All net poppers going on.

Shirts and skins mix it up,
Street wise tactics hanging tough.

Hooping in, Hooping out,
Hooping up, Hooping down.

Scoring high is my mission.
While talking trash to the opposition.

Pig Skin Sheep Skin

Senior year drug free,
Saving the games up to me.

Honeys watching from the stand,
Cheerleaders flipping to the band.

Caught the pigskin, and left skid marks,
The scout that saw me ignited the sparks.

Career shot off like a rocket,
Until I tore my knee out of socket.

All that cheese and the honeys are gone,
Now, I'm in this mansion all alone.

Getting back in school to get that sheepskin,
Got to pay back taxes no matter which team win.

Harlem Sweet Harlem

It's the roaring 20's after World War l.
Now it's time to have some fun.

Well dressed handsome gents with a sophisticated debutante,
Yeah Baby, we're in the mist of the Harlem Renaissance.

Sneaking in back of the Cotton Club to have a peek,
Pausing in the alley to take a leak.

Jazz is here and it sounds real good,
Weekend 'nights' bring other folks to the hood.

Fletcher, Fats and Duke are playing with joy.
We're lindy hopping at the Sugar Cane and stomping at the
Savoy.

Well, its getting late and I'm about to split the scene,
Uh oh, wait a minute there goes Sweet Mama Stringbean.

Hey! The Depression is over and so is World War II,
Guess I'll take a stroll down Lennox Avenue.

I'll Get a nice job 'cause of the President's New Deal Plan,
I's a good thing A. Phillip Randolph took a stand.

Oh yeah that's really quite true,
He forced Franklin to issue Executive Order 8802.

Gotta catch Lady Day at the club tonight,
Satchmo will be there from his Midwest flight.

This is the longest line I ever seen at the Apollo,
It's cold out here, but I can't butt I got to follow.

But this cold ain't nothing compared to Korea that night,
Getting a frostbitten foot took me out of the fight.

Unlike Korea, Nam didn't end very soon,
I shipped out after they shot Malcolm at the Audubon Ballroom.

I should go to the rally to Support the Panther 10,
But the brothers trying to take the rackets from the dagos want me in.

They've always taken a bite out of the dark side of the Big Apple,
Leaving what's left for us to fight over and grapple.

First, I'll take my girl out for some ribs and wings,
Then we can relax and discuss some things.

I'm never scared and I never quiver,
Not even when a gang threw me in the Harlem River.

Iraq on the other hand was a different situation,
The thing that shook me up was the anticipation.

No matter where I go or hang my hat,
This town has always been where it's at.

Even When listening to wanna be rappers chase Stardome,
Yeah, Baby, there's no place like Harlem.

Dr. Dean's Deserving

Dr. Dean was never sinister or frightening,
Yes, he shot thru my life like a bolt of lightning.

As sons of the same God he adopted me into his family tree.
So, I assumed God had me protecting him,
Until I realized God had him protecting me.

As I faltered and slumbered all alone,
He reached down, pulled me up and then he was gone.

Oh, Heavenly Father I know your time is not ours,
Yet it happened so fast I never presented him his flowers.

I know Dr. Dean was never concerned about that or anything else,
he was so righteously due.
His only concern was that I continue to present them to You.

Our Flag

The sun is red
The people are black,
The land is green.

Waving, waving and beckoning,
Do we dare approach?
We certainly don't need permission.

Or do we?

Soulful Sunday

Sunday afternoon, afta church,
Catfish fryin', Grandbabies cryin'.
Screen door keepin' the flies out.

The aroma of sweet potato pies coolin'
The sound of watermelon rind slittin'.
Square shaped cornbread waitin'
For fried chicken and collard greens datin'.

Dining room table adorin'
Wit rhythm and blues soarin',
No malt liquor present, no reefer smoke in the air,
This pleasantry is a family affair.
Dressed in our Sunday best,
Not only family, but friends and guest.

Before all the caddies, wagons and pintos go,
We must all take a photo.
Now that we've taken ah pictcha,
Here's a few plates to take witcha.

Dressed 2 Kill

Spit shined gators,
Wit ah stingy brimmed dobbs.

Dressed real spiffy,
Not like some slobs.

Tre' piece doubled breasted,
Pinstripe and mohair.

Leather gloves and walking cane,
Yeah, I'm in there.

Dark cashmere wit scarf slung 'round da collar,
Sportin' ah time piece dat costed top dollar.

Silk sox wit matchin' rayon boxers and dago tee,
Even undressed she's still gonna dig me.

If The Shoe Fits

Half of you'all part time gay and claim God is the Great Mother,
While the rest of you'all laughing, grinning, and killing each other.

You quit believing in God and that's a fact,
You only did it because Putin showed you that Jesus was black.

You wanna come at me, get in line,
You Snakes are dangerous, but you don't have a spine.

To show you don't have any bravery,
You fool's are willing to go back into slavery.

White Tongues, Black Thongs

The serpent seduced you again with his slithering tongue,
Like a french tickler, it took your breath away from each lung.

The pleasure it aroused influenced your politics.
You even donned heels and thongs to do their porn flicks.

We could have licked you and pleased you just the same.
But you would only respect us if we were a pimp or sold co-
caine.

Besides, eating the forbidden fruit was never part of our culture.
Dining down there is characteristic of a buzzard or vulture.

No one can turn a hoe into a housewife, and that's the truth.
The fact that you were flipped by a forked tongue is living
proof.

To Win You Back

Still thinking of you
Each and everyday.

Hoping what was started
Has not faded away.

If it's your heart that I've failed to win.
Then I've committed a dreadful sin.

And I must put your short memory on a shelf,
And figure out how to redeem myself.

I Want

I want to shower in rainbows with you
Until they flood the ground.
And shooting stars come raining down.

I want you to feel my vibrations,
Until they unlock your deepest sensations.

I want to hold you in my arms in the moonlight,
Until our soul's merge and take flight.

I want us to eat from the same tree.
I want to wake up and feel you next to me.

Red Black and Green

The red warmth of our closet star,
Nourishes green vegetation from afar.

Black bodies shower in its rays,
In valleys beneath rainbows and mountain haze.

Let's wrap ourselves in these colors
The same as others do ole' glory,
Listening not only to her voice,
But, also to her story.

Songbirds will add melody to our lyrical praise,
Unto the Heavenly Creator for the rest of our days.

Queen Goddess Henrietta

These are the undisputed facts,
Euro medical scientist stole the cells of Henrietta Lacks.

They built a multibillion-dollar empire off of our deceased Queen,
Without compensating her children or siblings anything.

Many were sadden and many shed tears,
After her brief thirty- seven years.

There was much hurt considering she left to soon,
And the aftermath poured much salt into that wound.

Now it is not only our duty but moral right,
To use our scholastic skills and intelligence,
To rid the world of such parasite.

Just as her cells are still immortal,
So is Goddess Henrietta,
By transitioning through a dimensional portal.

A Walk In The Park

Sun beams sparkling off of Lilly ponds,
While butterflies float over bushes.

The smell of barbeque filled the air,
The squirrels horseplay across the grass.

What a wonderful day for a walk in the park.

The tunes from ice cream trucks along the perimeter,
Muffled by the sounds of jazz and blues.

Such a wonderful day walking the park.

Feeding the ducks and geese unafraid to come near,
With birds joining in from a distance,
whispering melody through the air.

Just a wonderful day for a walk in the park.

Three Way Love

Beautiful mahogany eyes with smooth ebony skin,
A natural attraction for all masculine men.

Imagine me, you and God,
Such a love triangle is not odd.

Though we may believe love can merge our two souls into one,
Beloved, without God it can never be done.

Can I trust you with my heart?
Always and not just from the start?
Or would we someday grow apart?

Adam so passionately loved Eve,
Yet in return she chose to deceive.

Samson could move boulders and giant rocks,
Yet his love for Delilah costed him his locks.

Job was a man who had it all,
Yet left to his wife he would have been destined to fall.

Your voluptuous beauty may leave me weak in the knees,
Because you're so fine,
Yet, I can never allow you to leave me weak in the spine.

Loving you the wrong way will only bring about a chastening rod,
For I can never love anyone more than I love God.

Therefore, my Love it can only be,
God, you and me.

God Before Woman

Eve betrayed Adam,
Delilah betrayed Samson,
Elaine betrayed Huey.

Abraham resisted Sarah,
Job resisted too.

Now you do the math
And decide which path.

Feeling divine or a divine feeling?
Feel good sensation or a divine healing,

Before succumbing to physical lust,
through physical thirst,
Remember our God the Creator always comes first.

Never Far

Whenever I'm away,
Locked down or stationed overseas,
You're on my mind.

A consistent incentive, to endure hardship
With the thoughts of being reunited.

Images of us alone on a pollution free planet,
Swimming with dolphins in crystal clear waters,
Beneath light blue skies with ivory puff clouds and sunshine rays.

We walk afterwards through a rich green paradise,
Sprinkled with a rainbow of flowers.

Forever vigor and strong,
Two bodies becoming one,
Under dark blue skies with sparkling stars
And moonlit beams.

Still longing to be back together for eternity.

Dearest Daughter

Dearest Daughter
Love of my life,
Life of my love,
Blood of my blood.

Dearest Daughter
Soul of my heart,
Heart of my soul,
Best of my character.

Dearest Daughter
Angel of my faith,
Faith in my angel
Hope of my dreams.

Although our family was brief,
As a father my emotions and memories
Are intense enough to hold them forever,
Because you're my nearest, clearest and
Dearest Daughter.

Flower Love

Springtime breezes the beginning of her birth,
Nourished by rains that fall to the earth.

Breaking thru grass with greens stems looming,
Different colors and shapes are blooming.

Countryside mountains, meadows and open fields,
Backyard, parks and valley hills,

Hubbies bringing them home to beg her pardon,
Florist picking them from the shop's garden.

Bees are buzzing 'cause the pollen's sweet,
The fragrance that put lovers in heat.

Purple Plum

Dark and sweet, plump and round,
The mildest love ever found.

I searched for seasons near and far,
You're not the moon, but you are a star.

Fresh green leaves are your clothing,
Relieving yourself of them is not loathing.

Smooth as silk and soft as cotton,
A taste like yours is never forgotten.

I lie under your tree for you to drop,
Hoping to the heavens you'll never stop.

With the complexion of grapes, but more to offer,
Even purple inside, and much, much softer.

Sweet Georgia Peach

Cute red bone with Lucious lips,
A plump bottom, lean waist and wide hips,

Ripe 4 da pluckin' or wit yo delicious juices,
You may just fall down.

If I can't pluck u, then I'll scoop u from the ground,
'Cause I don't ever wanna see u down.

I ask dat u leave yo family tree holdin' my hand,
'Cause it's hard fallin' 2 da Georgia red clay, dirt and sand.

Diamond Eyes

Glittering, sparkling, glowing bright,
Twin crystals reflecting off the moonlight.

We're all alone on the beach before dawn,
Shoeless on the shores that have no lawn.

Your Illuminous rays will melt my heart,
If I can just look away it'll never start.

I believe that's so, it certainly seems,
Still, I'm captivated by those radiant beams.

But I can't let them cut my soul in half,
Even tho' they're incapable of even cutting thru glass.

I've seen enough of the sparkle I suppose,
So, I think it's time to keep them close.

Beautiful Sweet Alicia

Alicia is so sweet,
And she has the perfect physique,

Nearly six feet tall,
An ebony beauty with long hair and all.

No weave or extensions,
A bright smile and luscious lips not to mention.

With an hour glass figure that's the envy of most females,
Alicia is radiant down to her bright colored toenails.

She moves and represents with graceful elegance,
Matched only be her above average intelligence.

But world pressures to be ultra thin,
Has caused her to give in.

Dicting rcductions arc such a borc.
Because of them we may never see that beautiful body of Sweet Alicia anymore.

One can only hope that she'll quit,
And keep that beautiful body God blessed her with.

Ronda Sweet Ronda

The mere presence of Ronda is intensely warm and sweet,
Like the rays of the sun dispensing, it's heat.

Her hair is dark and shiny like that of a raven,
With bright teeth and sweet lips that Henry once had been craving.

Voluptuous and alluring for him to desire,
It was the love of Ronda that he had wished to acquire.

The sweetness of Ronda once captivated us all,
She got our attention, even if she didn't call.

No matter what she wore, she still was the neatest.
And to Henry, Ronda has always been the sweetest.

Mama's Day

Once a year it's Mama's Day,
It comes on a date in May.

Just as flowers begin to bloom,
Her children sneak into her room.

They know it's off limits and that's the rule,
But hiding a present there makes it cool.

Everyday is Mama's Day to them,
They just stick with tradition when they go out on a limb.

Even if it's something as simple as a card or tart,
She'll appreciate the fact that it comes from the heart.

Angels Descending

Dove winged beings landing among us,
To assist the King of Kings
Who departed two millenniums ago.

Bat winged creatures emerging
From the depths of the earth's bowels.

Brandishing plates of armor
From the spirit world they will come,
To do battle as mankind chooses.

Now visible to the earth realm
With stones removed and books opened,
Man's choice can never be clearer.

Slippin' Thru

Da cracks not wide enough
But I gotta slip thru.

Gotta greeze myself,
Gotta tease myself,
I gotta slip thru.

Times runnin' out,
Da ropes burnin',
I gotta get outta here.

Ah little motivation,
Wit much inspiration,
Is what'll make me move.

Know'n' whut's on da other side,
Or just, Knowin' whut I'm facing on this one.
Makes me wanna slip thru.

Black Cat

Black Cat cool,
Black Cat smooth,
Wit ah rap so cold,
it's been patented and sold.

Steppin' sharp thru inner city streets,
Mackin' da ladies between da sheets,
Dressed real slick form head 2 toe,
Lookin' like ah model at ah fashion show.

Black Cat down, Alway around,
Whether wearin' ah beret and raisin' ah fist,
He's promoting freedom while takin' ah risk.

The epitome of cool, suave and debonair,
Black Cats laid his rap everywhere,
Niarobi, Paris, Rio, Singapore and Macau,
He's even laying it in Mutha Russia now.

No matter where he's been round da globe,
Black Cat's always droppin' ah load,

Whether tall, short, phat, medium or slim,
It's still bad luck 2 cross in front of him.

Black Cat.

Holding It Down

Don't give them an excuse,
To inflict fatal abuse.

They wanna hurt you,
But I won't desert you.

I got yo back,
So quit bangin' and slangin' crack.

You're the youth that must be saved,
which most people hate,
Some of our own think it's 2 late.

Left up 2 them, from da womb you'd be euthanized,
Or for low grades in school, lobotomized.

Their conviction is strong and they won't waiver,
What you need now is ah Saint or da Savior.

Wit aggression and hatred poised from all around,
To hurt yourself would be ecologically unsound.

You're the youth that's hunted and hated da most,
But fear not, 'cause I'll never abandon my post.

Brotha Bangin' Brotha Slangin'

Brotha bangin', Brotha slangin',
Keepin' his people's heads rangin',

Kluckas managin' it,
Tellin' him he can't quit.

It's ah nice little rackit,
If you ain't on da back of it.

Kluckas can just say it's fratricide,
Pretending to be da heroes, on white horses they ride.

Saving us from what they're behind.
Da brothas don't see it 'cause they're blind.

He's lookin' at what he want stidda what he needs.
To git it he's sprinkling those crack seeds.

Killing other brothas to prove ah point.
Then lettin' da Kluckas put them in the joint.

Brotha Bangin' Brotha Slangin.

Sista Ho-in' Sista Blowin'

Sista ho-in' Sista blowin'.

Feedin' her habit stidda her child.
Captivated and fascinated wit dat lifestyle.

Doin' europes, getting' diseases,
Passin' 'em ta brothas as she sneezes.

On da triple x screen wearin' ah collar,
Sellin' her dignity 4 ah dollar.

Degrading herself just ta spite me,
If it's attention she wanted,
She coulda had it 4 free.

Sista went and cashed in her soul,
Just to impress me dat she could be bold.

Still, I'll definitely take care of da baby.
As 4 her well…maybe.

Sista ho-in' Sista blowin'.

White Lips, Black Hips

Goin' downtown wuz her thang, not yours,
If sisters did it they were called whores.

We were jest having fun, which made her the real whore,
Because we loved you much, much more.

It was mainly lust with little emotion,
But for your love we would swim an Ocean.

Why can't you understand what we've all gone through,
We only did it, to restore pride in honor of you.

The only joy I got from having that fun,
Was mocking them for what they did to you,
While holding me under the gun.

Friday Night Out

Cashed my check and paid my bills,
What's left tonight is 4 my thrills.

I worked hard all week and pushed it to da max,
Now it's time to kick back and relax.

Sit at da bar, sip some suds and listen to da groove,
Afta dat I'll git up on da dance flo and move.

I'm off tomorrow so what da hell,
No work or overtime Saturday, So I'll stay a spell.

I'll do it again tomorrow nite, but not so late.
Gotta git up Sunday Morning to attend service,
Before dey pass da plate.

Hot Work   Hard Work

Education 4 what?
Are u some kind of nut?

To work da sugah cane fields,
Ya don't need no classes.
It's ta produce sugah 4 my rum and molasses.

It don't take much 2 know how 2 pick cotton,
There's ah whip behind you in case you've forgotten,

I know it's not fair,
'Cause it's hot out there.

Hell, I'm on the porch sipping ice tea,
And it's still hot out here to me.

Daddy's Week

Working two jobs to feed every kid,
Daddy wasn't ashamed of nothing he did.

Hard work builds character and rightfully so.
He hoped to leave us something so we'd know.

Weekends he took us to ball games and church.
Sometime he'd stop to buy from salesmen peddling merch.

www.ingramcontent.com/pod-product-compliance
Ingram Content Group UK Ltd.
Pitfield, Milton Keynes, MK11 3LW, UK
UKHW041316190726
13845UKWH00025B/301

9 788119 654116